Trailhead Publishing
Colorado, USA

2025

TRAILHEAD PSALMS

Field Notes for the Formerly Lost

D. Blake Washington

A collection of poems about reclamation, memory,
and the quiet wilderness of becoming

For Mom,

The root beneath all my wandering.
Worried I'd lose the path,
but never once let go of the thread.

Contents

Invitation

Come as you are—
boots muddy, breath short,
carrying what you haven't learned
to set down yet.
These are field notes
from the territory
between lost and found—
not a map, but proof
the trail exists.
Start wherever
your feet touch ground.

Artifacts and Inheritance

Reclaiming a Hand-Me-Down Body

I.

This body was issued, not chosen.
Stitched from hospital linen,
red dirt dust,
and stories I was too young to question.

The knees came from an uncle
who ducked when things got loud.
You don't inherit knees like these from peace.

The shoulders were built for lifting
other people's guilt.
The chest for bracing,
not breathing.

Even the silence feels inherited.
Handed down like a family Bible—
worn at the edges,
heavy in the wrong places,
never opened all the way.

II.

There's a boy in me
who learned stillness early.
Hands folded,
jaw locked.

Praised for his posture,
no one asked
why his spine never loosened.

He learned fast
that softness drew questions,
and questions carried consequences.

So he stayed neat.
Stayed quiet.
Kept his sadness
pressed flat like a church shirt,

crease sharp as the day it was folded.

III.

I took this borrowed body
into the woods.
Not for healing,
but to stop leaving pieces of it behind.

No welcome,
no blessing,
no call to my name.
The trail simply was.

The trees didn't care
for a label or diagnosis.
The stones didn't ask
what I'd do next.

Shame unpacked itself quietly—
like a guest who'd stayed too long
but couldn't find the door.

I asked him to sit.
And I sat beside him
until we both stopped shaking.

IV.

The ache found a rhythm.
That was the first mercy.
Nothing changed but my gait,
steady enough to keep going.

I was walking,
and the ground no longer felt
like a test.

Some truths live under the skin,
in the breath,
in the way your shoulders finally stop
curling forward,
in how your chin lifts
when no one's watching.

V.

I stood at the summit
without chorus or sudden light,
just wind moving through me
like I wasn't in the way.

In that time and place,
the quiet felt endless.

A breath I'd been holding
for years let go.

I stayed myself,
but the man I was
fell in step beside me,
no longer a stranger.

I'm still here—
not healed,
but listening.

Not whole,
but walking.

And that,
despite everything,
feels like a beginning.

Lessons From the Father

I learned about him in fragments.
A name and a heritage, a sister, a brother.
A man who stayed when it counted.

None of his fragments whole,
but none of them small.
All but one of them loud.

Each a lesson I didn't know I was carrying
until I heard myself
giving it to someone else.

I've seen love held like a fist.
Silence used
to keep a house from splitting.

Been hugged by men who taught me nothing,
and ignored by men who taught me everything.

It all counted.
It all made it in,
with no bitterness now.

I'm just a man learning to be better than the blueprint.
Even the good parts—
the ones I still keep in my pocket,
warm from the walk,
heavy enough to remember
but not enough to weigh me down.

I don't call it anything
but human.
Disjointed.
Incomplete.
Enough.

Interlude

Bloodline

We are not a talkative people. We grunt, nod, and pretend not to notice the price. We survive some things by not speaking; certain sins keep their shape because we never name them. Our grief clocks in on time; our fear has dirty soles; tenderness, when it shows, hides inside advice.

We don't mention the drinking or the apologies that never made it out of the throat. We carry them instead—in liver, in jawline, in our hands, in the way our boys learn to wince before they ask.

I am still like them, still learning to say what the body already knows. So when the silence swells, I write. Maybe that isn't fully healing, but it helps to break the echo.

Unclaimed Baggage

I didn't pack light.
Never knew I could.

Most of it wasn't mine.
A tone of voice,
a scowl,
a stubbornness I took on
like a middle name.

Some of it looked like strength.
Some of it looked like love.
Some of it looked like leaving early
and calling it wisdom.

I carried secrets
like they were sacred.
I carried apology
like it was earned.

I carried the way men speak
without saying anything.
I carried the urge to explain
what should've been felt.

I carried bruises
like badges,
and tenderness
like contraband.

But I didn't ask for any of it.
The labels unread.
The bag unopened
until it was too heavy to lift
without gritting my teeth.

Now
I do the inventory.
I name what I brought.
I set down what isn't mine.

And whatever's left—
even the strange,
even the sharp—
that's mine now.

I'll carry it all,
this time,
with purpose.

Field Note: no-moon house

power out; house stops humming.
bare feet on cold floor, listening edge-first.
not the center—just a body.

Field Note: old fencepost

leaning, splintered.
still holding the shape
of what it divided.

The Long Walk In

Men Who Cry in Trucks

They don't talk much about it.
That's not silence,
it's frame.

You learn early how to hold your gaze
when the blood swells.
How to keep a steering wheel steady
with a tremor in your hands.

Some men disappear in bars.
Some in bedrooms.
Some in the middle of a sentence.

But some go to their trucks—
alone, parked, engine off—
where the air never asks questions
and the rearview mirror
knows better than to look.

You'll see them sometimes
just sitting there.
Long after the fight ended,
long after the phone call,

not doing anything.

Which is exactly how you know
something's happening.

Grief doesn't come in sobs.
It shows up
like heat from the vents.
Slow at first,
then everywhere.

There's a peacefulness
in letting it fall
in a place that never asked
to hold it.

They'll wipe their faces,
turn the key,
and drive off like nothing changed.

But the seat remembers.
And so do they.

I Was Built to Carry Things

That's all anyone ever needs from me.
Weight, mostly.
Sometimes people.
Sometimes silence.

I don't ask where we're going
or what broke.
I just make sure we get there
and keep quiet
when we don't.

Sometimes he stays long after the key turns.
Lets the cold settle in.
Lets the quiet
unmake a little more of him
than the world allows.

I've seen hands
grip a wheel like a lifeline.
Watched men
let it all fall
where no one would see.

Except me.
And I don't tell.

It's not much,
but I know the shape of grief
when it leans back in the seat
and forgets
how to leave.

I don't need thanks.
Or meaning.
Or a name.

I was built to carry things.
That's all.

And I never said
he had to carry it alone.

Field Note: mule deer

ears first, then the rest of the sentence.
we read each other and decided to pass.

Interlude

January Couch

It was someone else's couch in mid-January, after I'd said too much and no one told me I was too much. Cheap fleece that smelled of lavender and dog. The fridge hummed in the kitchen. For once, I could exhale without rehearsing.

I stayed quiet and asked for nothing. The room held me without conditions. I remember that night—being allowed to exist without explaining; the fridge still humming; the blanket rough at my wrist like it wanted to know my name.

Instructions for My Body if I Don't Make It Back

Don't clean it up.

Let the dirt speak.
Let the sweat stay.
If the knees are bent, leave them like that—
I was probably resting.
Or remembering.
Or letting go of something I never got to say.

Don't fold my hands.
They were never good at stillness.
Let them rest open,
like I was reaching for something
but chose not to force it.

If the trail kept going,
follow it until the light shifts.
If it ends at a tree,
sit there.
Whatever I found—
it's somewhere in the quiet.

Don't bring flowers.
Bring silence.
Bring worn boots with tread.
Bring a boy who hasn't yet learned
it's okay to feel more than one thing at a time.
Let him carry one of my stories—just one.
He'll know which.

Don't say I was brave.
Say I was learning.
Say I walked farther than planned,
and by the end,
the weight I carried
finally felt like mine.

If you find my body,
know that it was mine.
At the end,
it was finally mine.

What the Fire Forgot

It took the shed.
The photo albums in the bottom drawer.
My high school jacket with the stitched-on names
no one ever called me.
It took the doorframe I once measured myself against
before I quit growing.

It took the porch.
The place we said things we couldn't inside.
The swing.
The splinters.
The ash from cigarettes we wouldn't admit we smoked.

But it missed a few things.

The way my stomach drops when someone slams a cabinet.
The sound my stomps make when I leave angry.
The pit I fall into when I'm trying not to cry.
The laugh I inherited but rarely use.

It didn't get the part of me that rebuilds
without asking anyone to notice.
The slow heat I carry in my chest
that isn't rage,
just the last warm thing
no one ever put out.

The fire forgot
that not all damage is visible.
That not everything that burns
is gone.

It forgot
how many things are built from what remains.
That new growth smells like smoke
for a long, long time—
and still it grows.

Field Note: peregrine falcon

air folds around a fast idea.
speed writes its own permission slip.
the cliff signs off without blinking.

Field Note: mountain lion

quiet gold in the treeline.
you don't see it—
you feel seen.

Natural Witnesses

Field Note: black-billed magpie

confetti in a suit. side-eye like a mirror.
a thief, sure—of the shiny and the unguarded.

At the Creek

It moved
like it always had.
Like it would keep moving
whether I showed up or not.

I was hunting for a place
quiet enough
to think all the way through.

The rocks were slick.
The water was cold,
honest.

I stood for a while,
trying to remember the last time
I let my body rest
without apology.

Then I dropped to my knees
because some things
are easier to face
when you're closer to the ground.

The creek had no answers,
no speech about worthiness.
It just moved around me,
laughing.

Moss Has Memory, Too

It never seems to want attention.
Just shows up
where something once fell
and stayed a while.

You can clear a trail for years
and still find moss
covering what you thought
you buried properly.

I've seen it take root
on old stones,
forgotten tools,
and the edges of graves
no one visits anymore.

And I've felt it, too—
soft as regret,
cold as a truth you meant to outgrow
but didn't.

People talk about plants turning to light.
Moss turns to rot.
Turns toward what's left behind.
Doesn't expect it to be better.
Just covers it gently
until it stops needing to be explained.

There's a kind of wisdom in that.
The kind you warm yourself by
without knowing why.

I think the body recalls the same way—
in patches,
in damp corners,
in places we forgot to clear
because it hurt too much
to touch again.

And if healing comes at all,
it won't be loud.

It'll feel like a witness who never speaks
but never leaves,
guarding the shapes
of things that fell.

Sky as Alibi

I looked up
so I wouldn't have to explain myself.

Called it wind.
Called it cold.
Let the sky take the blame.

Clouds don't press.
They change shape the way moods do;
no ledger, no tally to keep.
They just pass,
always headed somewhere else.

When I couldn't find the words,
I stared into that open blue
and let it speak for me—
not in poetry—
in space.

No one questions you
when you're looking at the sky.
They assume you're thinking,
or somewhere far off.

And maybe I was.
Maybe I am.

But the sky gave me cover
on days I couldn't be brave—
held the weight of what I wouldn't say
and never wanted it back.

Once, I watched a hawk
redraw my alibi
one circle at a time.
Never pressed, just passing.

Maybe it's not really healing,
just one more way
to survive unnoticed.

But some days,
that's the only kind that works.

Field Note: ponderosa pine

bark like dried rivers; crown snagged in the sky.
fog threads the branches and leaves the questions whole.
older than my names—stillness outlasts us both.

If the Fences Failed

I wasn't raised in the wild, but the body doesn't lie. It learned what it needed in silence. Learned to crouch at the first crack of a voice too sharp. Learned the way wind smells before a change. Hackles rise easy but not without reason. Fangs remember things I've never spoken, and maybe never will.

There are places in me still unschooled. Uncivilized. Untamed. Legs that move before thought arrives. Shoulders that close like stone. I've mistaken an open palm for a blow more than once. Yet some part of me still reaches for it. Not out of hope, maybe, but out of the same instinct that draws a cold animal to fire.

They call it trauma. They call it lineage. I don't bother with names. What I know is that it runs deeper than memory. That it lives in the twitch of bone, in breath held without noticing, in the way I scan a room when I enter. Folded beneath posture and good manners. Fragmented like old songs you only remember in dreams.

I've dreamed of wolves. Not the ones with glass eyes and bedtime teeth. The kind that watch from the dark and never blink. Heavy things. Sacred. Still. I've felt them move inside me. In the tendons. In the chest. That quiet part that sees blood and doesn't tremble.

The wild dressed itself in patience. Walks quiet. Wears restraint like a clean shirt. When I walk now, alone, I catch the scent of something that was mine long before I knew language. Something older than grief. Older than men.

This body knows—how the elk fled, the line of least resistance. Instinct knows which fence will fail when it counts. Like pronghorn reading wire with their knees, I practice where it gives.

> My body isn't broken; it wasn't meant to stay leashed this long. It's already moving toward something I won't name—not until the wind speaks first.

Field Note: sentinel prairie dog

one chirp splits the meadow in half.
somebody has to watch the sky.
today it's him. tomorrow, maybe me.

Interlude

Watchtower

Someone was always keeping lookout. Sometimes it was a boy too young to understand what he was guarding against. Sometimes it was a man whose silence stretched farther than his courage. We called it safety—this habit of waiting at the edge, scanning horizons no one else noticed—but safety was just another way of saying don't get caught.

I watched shadows lengthen while my body rehearsed how to vanish. I learned the sound of boots on gravel, the way a slammed door could echo for miles inside me. Up there, eyes wide, I wasn't protecting anyone. I was only protecting myself from being the one surprised.

The watchtower was never high enough to see peace coming. Only trouble, and the memory of it arriving again and again.

Quiet Returns

Sanctuary

The trail kept going.
Worn-in. Unbothered.
A line drawn by every foot
that needed to leave something behind.

I've backtracked on this path before.
Looking for signs.
Trying to name the exact place
it all started to hurt.

But the dirt doesn't archive.
The ridges can't remember
why I turned around last time.

There's no memorial to my shame out here.
Wildflowers.
Wind.
A path that says,
Start wherever your breath catches.
Every arrival is a return,
even when you don't recognize the place.

It took me too long to realize
I was the only one still telling the story
of who I used to be.

The way forward didn't hold it against me.
Didn't hold anything but space.

Enough to walk.
Enough to fall.
Enough to keep going.

Field Note: tiger salamander

black with lantern stripes, storm-born.
the earth remembered rain
by giving it a body.

Rewritten in Spring

I came back to the same trail
with a different kind of reverence.
Not the heavy kind,
the listening kind.

The notes I left last season
are still here—
in the way I slowed at certain turns,
in the pauses I didn't name.

I never crossed them out
or cleaned the page.
I wrote between the lines.

Today, I noticed a type of bird I missed last time.
A breeze that no longer stung.
A stone I once tripped over
felt smaller somehow.

I'm not sure if I changed
or if the rocks softened.
But something gave,
and I settled in.

Maybe healing isn't erasure.
Maybe it's re-entry.
Maybe it's standing in the same place
with less weight on your back
than ever before.

I used to catalog the damage.
Now I notice the bloom.

Not everything is new,
but some of us are.
Still becoming, still bending
toward whatever light
the trees haven't learned to block.

Field Note: ember

ring of ash still warm.
what stays after the leaving keeps its heat.
patient fire under gray.

After the Rain, Home

The street, still wet,
held the shape of the storm
in shallow mirrors.
I stepped over them like I might wake something.

A black bird shook itself dry on a wire.
Somewhere, a gutter still carried the last of it away.

I slowed my pace.
Let the smell in the air remain unnamed,
the clouds unaccounted for.

It was enough to watch
how the world took water,
held it for a while,
and then let it go.

Field Note: no one watching

doorway left open; nothing to close.
past the bend where names stop meaning.
between grassline and first shadow, the air thins;
the calls fade to a whisper.

Field Note: green volunteer

thin shoot through cracked concrete.
unwatered, unasked—reaching for light.
soft and stubborn; still here.

Unspoken Benedictions

How to Be a Man without Disappearing

Start by noticing where you flinch.
Not in pain.
In habit.

Where you apologize for needing.
Where you swallow whole sentences
to keep the room from shifting.

Then notice who taught you that.
And ask if they ever looked free.

Being a man isn't vanishing.
It's not shrinking to keep everyone else
comfortable in your silence.

It's not carrying everything
just because your hands are bigger.

It's asking, without shame,
for the kind of love
you were never shown.

It's telling the truth
even when it comes out jagged.

It's letting softness live
in your face,
in your voice,
in your open palms.

You don't have to trade gentleness
for grit.
You don't have to break things
to prove your strength.

Some days, being a man
is just staying
when leaving would be easier.

Some days,
it's letting yourself be seen
without performance,
without armor.

And if that feels impossible,
remember this:
you are not the first boy
who mistook disappearing
for becoming.

But you can be the last
in your line
to unlearn it.

The One I Couldn't Keep

He was tired,
but he called it weakness.
Tired in the way some of us get
when we stop believing
the exits are real.

I see him sometimes
in the way I hit the light switch
twice.
In the way I go quiet
when the room turns kind.

He knew how to perform.
He knew the rules.
But he never learned how to unlearn
what kept him alive.

I left him in a year I don't name.
Buried him under,
Just a phase,
I'm good,
Don't worry, I've got it handled.

But I still hear him
at the edge of sleep.
Tapping.
Asking if I remember
what we almost did.

I do.

I remember the bridge.
The bottle.
The silence.
The way the mirror seemed to flinch.

He wanted rest.
Not saving.

Maybe I'm not better.
But I got up.

I got up,
and I didn't go back.

That's all.

I carry his voice
more like a warning
than a secret.

Psalm for the Boy

You weren't supposed to make it
because I kept pretending
you didn't exist.

I dressed you in black.
Taught you how to brace.
Taught you how to vanish inside a room
by taking up just enough space to pass.

I told you love had to be earned.
Told you tenderness was a trick.
And when you cried,
I looked away
like shame couldn't be trusted.

But you stayed too.

Tucked into the corners
of my laughter,
my chaos,
my loneliest nights.

You stayed
even when I claimed your softness
was the thing that nearly ruined me.

I see now,
it wasn't.

It was the thing that kept me
from becoming someone
I wouldn't recognize.

So this is for you.

Not an apology
or a fix.
A hand outstretched
toward the part of me
that never stopped hoping
I'd remember.

You made it,
and I'm still learning how to be someone
you'd be proud to grow into.

Start Where It Breaks

You don't need a plan.
You don't need to fix it first
or name the wound
before you start walking.

Just notice
where it cracked,
where the voice shook.
Where the ground dropped out
from under what once felt solid.

That's the place.

Where you flinched and stayed silent.
Where you left and called it strength.
Where you stayed too long
and called it love.

Start there.

You don't need to be ready,
just honest.
Be willing to put one foot
in front of who you used to be.

The map doesn't matter
if the breath is real.

Start where it breaks.

Where you bent and kept bending.
Where something in you said,
I can't do this anymore.
And something else said,
Do it anyway.

With the smell of dust lifting after rain
and your hands still open
from whatever you dropped to get this far.

That's the trailhead.
Not marked, not paved,
but yours.

Walk it.
Even if your legs shake.
Even if your voice does too.

You don't need to become someone else.
Just someone who keeps going.

Start where it breaks.
Trailhead begins here.

Field Note: coyote

dust at the ankles, maps in the blood.
every fence was a suggestion.

nothing waits at the edge
but hunger.

Field Note: raven

black wing in the margin,
voice like a cracked bell.

the sky was never empty,
only waiting to be read.

Acknowledgments

*This book was written in the company of shadows, stress &
silence, and all the things that didn't kill me but still shaped the
way I walk.*

*I thank my friends, my family, the forests and mountains, and
the long walks that teach me how to be with myself.*

*To Dallas Henry, my loyal companion—thank you for carrying
me into this new life with more confidence than I could ever
muster alone.*

*To the ones I've loved and lost, in every form—you are part of
this, even if you never knew it.*

And to you, the reader: thank you for meeting me here.

Author's Note

This work was created independently and represents
the author's personal reflections.

www.ingramcontent.com/pod-product-compliance
Lightning Source LLC
Chambersburg PA
CBHW031441120626
46545CB00006B/2515